WHAT THE RAVEN SAID

DATE DUE

PRINTED IN U.S.A.

Books by Robert Alexander

White Pine Sucker River: Poems 1970-1990
(New Rivers Press, 1993)

Five Forks: Waterloo of the Confederacy
(Michigan State University Press, 2003)

What the Raven Said
(White Pine Press, 2006)

Anthologies Edited by Robert Alexander

The Party Train: A Collection of North American Prose Poetry
(New Rivers Press, 1996)

The Talking of Hands: Unpublished Writing by New Rivers Press Authors
(New Rivers Press, 1998)

WHAT THE RAVEN SAID

ROBERT ALEXANDER

WHITE PINE PRESS / BUFFALO, NEW YORK

White Pine Press
P.O. Box 236
Buffalo, New York 14201
www.whitepine.org

Acknowledgments

The author wishes to thank the editors of the following magazines, in which some of
these poems first appeared: *Luna, Washington Square, The Prose Poem: An International Journal,*
Flyway, and *Sentence.*

Cover illustration: "Sable Lake," by Maeve Croghan, from the personal collection of
the author.

Publication of this book was made possible, in part, with public funds from the
New York State Council on the Arts, a State Agency.

First Edition.

10-digit ISBN: 1-893996-76-X
13-digit ISBN: 978-1-893996-76-2

Printed and bound in the United States of America.

Library of Congress Control Number: 2006923279

for Katie

A while since the croaking of the pond-frogs and the first white of the dog-wood blossoms. Now the golden dandelions in endless profusion, spotting the ground everywhere. The white cherry and pear-blows— the wild violets, with their blue eyes looking up and saluting my feet, as I saunter the wood-edge—the rosy blush of budding apple-trees— the light-clear emerald hue of the wheat-fields—the darker green of the rye—a warm elasticity pervading the air—the cedar-bushes pro- . fusely deck'd with their little brown apples—the summer fully awaken- ing—the convocation of black birds, garrulous flocks of them, gather- ing on some tree, and making the hour and place noisy as I sit near. . . .

As I write, I am seated under a big wild-cherry tree—the warm day temper'd by partial clouds and a fresh breeze, neither too heavy nor light—and here I sit long and long, envelop'd in the deep musical drone of these bees, flitting, balancing, darting to and fro about me by hundreds—big fellows with light yellow jackets, great glistening swelling bodies, stumpy heads and gauzy wings—humming their per- petual rich mellow boom. (Is there not a hint in it for a musical com- position, of which it should be the background? some bumble-bee symphony?) How it all nourishes me, lulls me, in the way most needed.

—Walt Whitman

CONTENTS

Three: What the Raven Said

One:
Ralph Goes to the Birds

The Ice Is Gone from the Lake

The ice is gone from the lake now—blown to the east, to the large open water of the main part of the lake—when I take my dog for a walk in the still evening air, the lake before me barely rippled, wavelets slapping at the ice-free rocks along the shoreline.

The ducks have returned, or at least one has, a female mallard, keeping to her distance thirty feet or so from my dog on her leash. (You can't be too careful around dogs if you're a duck, I suppose.) This duck is slowly paddling back and forth in a small cove, and at occasional intervals she lets go with a forlorn-sounding bleat. I pause by the picnic table to watch the fading red clouds and the pale blue water. The duck slowly makes her rounds. A male duck comes flying by through the twilight, and the duck in the water lets out an abrupt series of squawks much louder than her previous low sounds. She is so loud that my dog is startled and lifts her head from beneath the picnic table where she's been grazing for scraps . . . and the drake wheels about in the air, doing a large U-turn as he descends to the water. He lands a foot or so away from the female and hesitates for a moment as though keeping a respectful distance. After a quick exchange of some sort—it's too dim for me to see clearly—he paddles to her side, and together they go off into the darkness.

Did they know each other beforehand? Perhaps they're long-time mates, and he was delayed somehow at the end of their migration, blown off course in a recent storm. Or perhaps they were strangers until this moment—and she cried out in the twilight for someone passing by, just looking for a place to spend the night.

Ralph in His Canoe

The sandpipers are back, bobbing up and down on nearly-submerged rocks by the shore, flying by Ralph (in his canoe) with their odd, downward-curving wings. The loons are all gone now from the lake, heading north for the summer. It's been raining this morning, a steady drizzle; a slight breeze ruffles the water. Up along the shoreline Ralph sees a single flowering crabtree, its blossoms like small explosions of light. In the water still lucid with spring Ralph catches a quick sight of a carp before it swims away, a murky shape longer than his forearm.

As Ralph rounds Second Point it stops raining, though the clouds remain. Soon Ralph finds himself in a flock of swallows swooping and weaving through a swarm of mayflies. Ralph has often seen these birds actually dip into the lake to catch their dinner, then shake themselves off and launch themselves upward in one motion—but today they never touch the water.

A cloud of swallows surrounds Ralph as he lifts his paddle and floats, motionless, upon the flat gray surface of the bay.

Ralph Goes to the Birds

It's the first hot day of the year, the trees a lime-green mist across the hills. Ralph's wife has left for the city and Ralph goes out to play guitar on the porch. An American plum is a splash of white on the hillside—the grass in the pasture is already green. By the porch the mountain ash has bare limbs through which Ralph can see the green hillside.

As Ralph sits playing it starts to rain—rain pours off the porch roof, rain in torrents bends the grass in the pasture. In a while the rain slows and stops, the sky clears, but Ralph keeps playing the same slow tune, trying to get it right.

The barn swallows soon appear with the sun to eat the spring's first crop of bugs—they flit in and out through the porch and Ralph's surprised at how close they come. Finally Ralph gets tired of playing, puts his guitar back in the case, and sits watching the sun on the lime-green hills and green fields, the puffy clouds of the first hot day of the year.

Suddenly two swallows are flying straight at Ralph. Abruptly they stop, hovering in front of him, twittering back and forth like teenagers in a school parking lot. Then just as suddenly, they fly off, and as Ralph sits startled one of the swallows reappears, gliding by him to perch on a thick porch beam—and for a long moment the bird looks back at Ralph.

In a Month This Will All Be

I followed my own trail here.
—Gary Snyder

Ralph comes down over the crest of the ridge, limestone outcrop-pings, the sun hot in May. Ralph's dog runs through the woods, a flash of black and white he can see through the small green leaves. In a month this will all be overgrown. Here's a small cave eroded back under the ridgetop, just large enough to crawl into out of the rain (though it's sunny today) and next to it an opening surrounded by fallen rock, just about large enough for a dog to lie down in.

Climbing around the thick oak that blocks the front of the cave, Ralph sees almost in the center of the circle of rocks a fragment of white bone, a leg bone perhaps of some small animal, finger-size, bleached white over the years—chewed on, Ralph sees, looking closer, picking it up, by several different sets of teeth.

He'd been walking down over the ridge into the valley, a warm spring day, and caught in a sudden thundershower, crawled in under the limestone to wait out the rain. His dog lay nearby in the rocks, chewing a bone he'd brought for her, as he dozed off to the sound of rain on the oak leaves—ten thousand years ago, yesterday.

The Naming of Muskrat Point

Early morning, and the water is flat, unruffled. In the shallows, spawning carp swirl and thrash. At times one raises himself nearly out of the water, muscles tense and glistening, the long fish arched in passion. Just down from where the cliffs run back into the hillside, there's flowering hawthorn, white flowers flowing to the water's edge like a bridal train.

From twenty-two miles above, a NASA photograph of Madison shows Lake Mendota, Picnic Point and Second Point clear as thumb and first finger of a giant's hand—and what's even clear on a close look is that Second Point isn't one, but two small promontories separated by a stretch of curving shoreline.

By a trick of morning sunlight, as I round the first of these small headlands—going east, facing open water—I'm invisible to a muskrat swimming up along the shoreline just the other side of a large rock. (Muskrats, I've noticed, seem quite nearsighted in the open air, though perhaps under water they are Deadeye Dicks.) At first I don't see this creature, but rather a bit of greenery—a sprig of basswood leaves, on closer look—moving along the shoreline. Immediately I stop paddling, and the muskrat, blinded perhaps by the glare of the low morning sun, continues to swim toward me.

As I watch, drifting only slightly on the flat water, I see the animal turn and swim into a dark spot between two rocks just at the end of the promontory, perfectly hidden by a willow tree that's collapsed across the rocks into the water and is still leafing out. It's only by the slightest chance that I see the entrance to this muskrat den. (On future days I will confirm the comings and goings of the muskrats—two of them, I learn: one morning I see one enter the den with some young willow leaves and, moments later, a smaller one emerge.)

Every Day Ralph

Every day since his divorce was final, Ralph puts his canoe in the water. First he must take his canoe out of the cave-like "boathouse" the previous owner built out of limestone and mortar at the base of the cliff, just high enough for Ralph to stoop over in—a dirt floor usually moist and sometimes, when the lake is high, puddle-deep in water—and wide enough for a rowboat. Ralph has been told by a neighbor that the professor used to camp out here by the lake when his wife was mad (angry perhaps that her husband was spending such long hours in the laboratory, returning after dinner to check on his experiments, then coming back to the lake to spend the night amidst the rustling of the oaks, the bright stars over the water). Dank it is, the boathouse, though more than large enough for Ralph's canoe. Often he sees, in the bottom of his canoe, a daddy longlegs, or several, for a multitude thrive there in the damp confinement of the boathouse.

Today Ralph leaves the daddy longlegs undisturbed in the bottom of his canoe. For the story goes like this: Just a year ago, out on the water one evening to watch the sunset, Ralph is startled by the soft touch of insect feet on his face and reaches up to brush the thing away—and brushes as well his glasses, which falling through the water fade quickly before he can even think not to move lest he capsize—leaving him, this Fourth of July weekend, unable to drive north for his vacation. . . .

And so, in due fashion, awaiting his new glasses, Ralph is still around town when his wife returns from a business trip to Australia. For a week, recovering, as she says, from jet lag, she's awake at night wandering around the house while Ralph sleeps alone in their double bed, hearing the sounds of old Joni Mitchell songs drifting up from the living room. When he awakens in the morning she is asleep on the couch and the bottle of scotch stands nearly empty. Finally, the evening before he leaves to drive north, dinner on the table, the sun setting behind a mystical screen of oh-so-slightly-moving basswood leaves, she announces she's in love with another man.

Ralph, out in his canoe in the morning light of another season, feels gratitude to the daddy longlegs in the bottom of his canoe. Had he left on time for vacation, she would perhaps (as so often in the past) have buried the truth beneath a veneer of lies . . . and he might, so he thinks, still be married to her, and not have met the woman who's become his lover—(but that's another story).

So every day, since his divorce, Ralph puts his canoe in the water. In the morning light he takes the daddy longlegs for a ride. Together they glide on the wide flat lake, clouds and water, blue sky and sun. *Thank you, Brother Longlegs* . . . Ralph breathes steadily, his paddle moving in his hands.

The Night the Honey Locusts Bloom

Late one night at the beginning of June, the honey locusts at the end of Ralph's street begin to bloom. That night, walking his dog, when he turns the corner at the end of the block he's swept by a sweet exotic fragrance, delicate as the perfume his lover wears at bedtime. Back and forth Ralph walks to find the exact spot beneath the trees—at least a dozen, he's counted them—which blossom on the same evening (a sign, he has read, that the trees are a single clone). Ralph stands there with his dog, taking deep breaths through his nose, trying to prolong the sweet smell of the honey locusts. In a day or two, he knows, their dry flowers will fall—and lie alongside the street like the first snows of autumn.

Duck Saga

From the hill about half a mile from my house, you can look out over Lake Mendota, facing north toward the narrow head of the lake where the Yahara River flows in. Years ago, before the trees grew up around this spot, the tribe that lived in this vicinity put up an effigy mound (a turtle pointing north, with a large boulder, a so-called glacial erratic, marking the head) right at the top of the hill, from which it's still possible, when the leaves are off the trees, to see out over the lake, to see the Big Dipper turning through the night. Now more than a few trees and a city have grown up around this spot, but the lake and the Big Dipper are still out there.

At the foot of this hill, nearly two hundred feet down, the slope steepens with a final plunge into the lake, limestone cliffs that rise some thirty feet above the water. I pass by here each day as I canoe toward Second Point, and I've become familiar over time with the lichens and blackberry vines that cover the cliff face, which stretches about a hundred yards along the shoreline. At one spot about midway along, there's a small ledge, no larger than a shoebox, six or seven feet above the water.

One day toward the end of May—leaves and lilacs out, the air filled with the sweet smell of purple flowers—I'm paddling eastward past the limestone bluffs and find myself looking up into the eyes of a duck roosting on this ledge. The female is nearly hidden behind a screen of blackberry vines and flame-red columbine, beside a cedar whose roots grapple and hug the rock. She's squatting there surrounded by a small pile of gray duck down, motionless, looking out at the water and the billowing clouds (with the *slap slap slap* of the water on the undercut bluffs a lullaby through day and night).

I stop paddling. The duck looks down at me with some suspicion as I drift a few feet from her, but she doesn't move. The look in her eyes reminds me of how my dog looks at me when I come into the kitchen, unsure of my intentions, but hoping for the best.

For the next few weeks this duck is there each morning as I paddle past. (One time only she's gone, perhaps feeding herself or getting a drink of water, and I see that she's built a low nest of duck down on the ledge—which I hope slants somewhat inward so that the eggs won't, by accident, roll into the water.) Each morning she watches me as I pass by, and sometimes I see a drake nearby. My duck handbook says that as soon as the female mallard begins to brood her eggs, the male of the species, thinking his job is complete, leaves her to pursue other females, but I wonder if perhaps the mallard drakes are so brightly colored at mating time not solely to attract the females, but also, when the female is nesting, to catch the eye of potential predators and lead them away. It's certain, in any case, that this drake is sometimes close by, and the female sitting among rocks and weeds is nearly invisible unless she moves. It's only by chance that I happened to see her, since I was looking at the plants growing along the bluff and she was in my line of sight.

After several weeks I'm starting to wonder if her eggs will ever hatch. She seems listless and bedraggled—no doubt hungry, I think, as I've never seen her dabbling like the other ducks who seems to spend most of their time (when they're not sleeping or preening) feeding themselves. I worry about her. How much weight has she lost? Is she thirsty all the time? She rarely seems to move, and hardly opens her eyes as I pass by. One day there's a red-tail hawk in a tree overhead, so close I can see the speckles on his belly, and I wait patiently—my legs cramping in the canoe, morning sunlight filtering down through full-grown leaves—until the hawk flies off across the lake.

A couple of days before I plan to drive north, I stop in front of her to say my good-byes. I'm telling her how much I wish I could see the birth of her babies, and how I wish for her a healthy brood and no tragedy befalling the ducklings, when I realize I'm seeing, under one wing, a small fuzzy head. She swells her breast up and moves her wing slightly forward to hide the hatchling from my sight. I've read that ducklings can survive for a day or so after hatching without needing water or food, but that usually within a few hours the mother will lead them to food and water—so I wait around hoping to see the whole troop jumping off the ledge, or being pushed into the lake below. And a whole troop it is, I realize, for over time I see a head and then two and then three popping up behind a wing, as she tries to maintain order among the rambunctious crew and keep me from seeing her babies. I think of a houseful of little kids running wild on a rainy day.

Finally I realize that as long as I'm around, she won't leave the nest with them, that she's probably terrified I want to eat them all—and so, not wanting to worry or disturb her, I lift my paddle and with a swirl of water turn and head for home.

Vacation Notes

1)   Out on Lake Superior a fog bank rises in the purple distance. It's still cold here on the Point—lilacs blooming at the end of June.

2)   A starling nests over the front door. First morning there's a dead one at my feet, it looks like a miniature ostrich—hairless, stomach bulging like a fried clam.

3)   I won't ever see Lee Johnson again on the Old Seney Road. I used to pass him driving out to his camp somewhere on the Whitewash plains, a wizened face through the window of his pick-up, nodding or smiling, just the two of us on the dirt road through the woods—you hardly ever pass anyone else out there, sometimes a lost tourist going too fast.

4)   I buried my old dog's ashes up by the river on the high banks, next to a good-sized white pine on one side and on the other a huge old stump—high, in the breeze, overlooking the river.

5)   I spent the day there, looking out over the water and the forest, and as night began to fall a single gull flew down the valley, toward me and by me—cruising—just overhead, and down along the river toward Lake Superior.

Ralph Attends the Turtle Convention

Just days before the solstice, Ralph enters the spring-fed bayou, his canoe slipping through a narrow opening in the marsh. A sun-hot morning, and the air is perfectly still here in the circle of water surrounded by trees. Wild iris are violet along the shore. Water lilies, white and yellow, dot the surface of the water.

Ralph hears the *chung chung* of bullfrogs all around him. Dragonflies zip back and forth across the pond. There are turtles of all sizes—two inches to half a foot across, he reckons—resting on the logs at the edge of the pond, watching him as he drifts upon the water. He stops counting when he reaches a baker's dozen. Three turtles, particularly wary, slip back into the water—but the rest continue to watch him. After a time, he oh-so-slowly turns the canoe and, not lifting his paddle from the water, starts back to Sable Lake. The turtles do not move.

The next day Ralph returns to the bayou, and the turtles are gone.

Lake Solstice

Today's the solstice: mountain ash along the shore lift their white flow-erheads like candelabra. When I pass the mouth of Towes Creek, pad-dling steadily, an eagle flaps outward from the tallest spruce along the shoreline. As the eagle rounds the point ahead of me, a slight movement reveals a deer standing in the shallows. She looks upward for a moment as the eagle passes overhead, then slips back into the trees.

Eagle and Otter at Midsummer

—for Jim Harrison

It was the summer that fifty while pelicans appeared one Sunday morning just off Coast Guard Point, diving for whitefish as the fishermen strung out along the pier stopped what they were doing and gaped. The solstice was just days past, and there were hundred-knot winds in Minnesota that, presumably, blew the birds off their intended course to their summer home five hundred miles to the west of here.

Later that same day I went canoeing on Sable Lake and saw three eagles circling above me. I looked again a moment later and they were gone, too high for me to pick out against the bluest of skies. A fourth one stayed back in the crooked pine by the place I've begun to call Eagle Cove, so many times I've seen eagles there in one tree or another.

Now I've rounded the point and reach the spot, thick with wild iris, where I turn for home. I'm resting a moment or two, the paddle across my knees, absorbed by the silence of the evening, when I realize that for some time I've been hearing a *tsk tsk tsk* as though someone's trying to get my attention: *Hey, Bud, over here.* I turn and see an otter, head above the water, watching me. Then—having seen enough of this intruder—he drops back down and disappears beneath the surface of the lake.

Two:
Home Is Where the Art Is

In the Sportsman

In the Sportsman Restaurant, old photos line the wall on either side of the huge brick fireplace—photos from turn-of-the-century Grand Marais: old fishing boats, piles of raw lumber and white-pine boards, folks in dark suits and hats. Eating lunch in the cool dark bar, I see a crowd standing on the boardwalk in front of the old Hargrave & Hill general store, looking back across the dirt street at the photographer, who's standing pretty much where the soldier's monument is today. In the group of a dozen or so people, I see a dog that looks like my own— same size, same pattern of black and white, white paws, white muzzle, black ears and face and body. The dog watches the photographer across the street with his large portrait camera. My dog's standing there, what's most amazing, the same quizzical expression on her face—slightly sad, mortal, life all too short, looking across the street, in front of a store that nearly a century ago burned to the ground. . . .

Baby Eagle at the Beach

On this summer morning, the lake a looking-glass for the sun's hot eye, I'm watching the reflection of a dragonfly move back and forth across the water. The insect itself is invisible, caught in the shadows of the tree-line by the water. A pair of kingfishers, chattering along the shoreline, follow me as I canoe; a sandpiper weaves back and forth, low over the water, feeding on the same swarm of mayflies as the dragonfly I'm watching. When I reach Eagle Cove, I see (as I have for several days previously) an eagle in the crooked pine, perhaps guarding a nest close by. Though she's at rest, her wings are spread out, drooping at her sides to catch any faint breath of breeze, looking for all the world like a woman who, sitting legs apart on a porch swing on a steamy summer day, hikes her skirt up above her knees.

Two months later I see a baby eagle at nearly this same spot: a large bird the size of a raven, black feathers sprinkled with white, a black head and tail. I float offshore watching him, as he sits on a bare branch just above the water. He lets me drift closer, perhaps fifty feet away, peers at me curiously for several minutes. Then he begins to cry out, and doesn't stop until suddenly there's a whoosh of feathers and his mother lights next to him. I can see the silver shape of a fish pass between them, before she flies a few feet off and perches on a branch that touches the water. She drinks then, looking at me, and turns the other way to look down the lake. The fledgling has stopped his crying, and his mother flies off down the lake. After a time the youngster follows her, and then I see overhead another eagle, six-foot wingspread at least, circling above me.

Upstream

After she dies—her heart giving out finally on the hottest morning of this short northern summer—my dog appears to me in a dream: *Here's how I want you to remember me.* We've arrived in Michigan a month or so later than usual, windows open all night and the room still breathless in the morning. Now it's our first time out by the river, mid-afternoon, the sun high overhead. I'm sweating and my dog's panting. We work our way down to the spruce-and-fir thicket at the base of the high banks, the trees stunted by the near-constant shade of the larger pine upslope, then struggle through tag alder to the river, step by step so as not to trip over the entangled low branches. Finally we reach a sandbar exposed in the low summer river, and my dog wades out into the water, where she stops facing downstream—forest all around us, sky overhead, a light breeze fluttering the cool water. She turns around and looks back at me, grinning as dogs do.

She died at the height of summer, the daisies still in full bloom, smack in the middle of the two weeks of heat that reaches even here to Lake Superior. She died under a waxing moon on the day of the ancient Celtic festival of Lughnasa, the blueberries now fully ripe across the high sand plains. A few days later I find the exoskeleton of an insect, split up the back and empty, the creature having passed on to the next stage of its life—and I imagine that this is how we leave our bodies behind.

There's a stream which flows into Sable Lake on its eastern side, flowing down through a low ridge into the lake. On hot summer mornings, if you canoe by that spot, you will feel a cool breath of air moving downslope over the flowing water of the creek. I pause in my canoe and watch the play of light and shadow through the leaves green now at the height of summer. I think about my dog, freed from the husk of her creaking and ancient body, floating now in the cool air and, with ease and curiosity, beginning her journey upstream.

Ralph among the Lily-Pads

Leaves all green and shiny screen the morning sun as Ralph sits in his canoe among the water lilies, and dragonflies scoot overhead. Suddenly a tadpole slithers onto a lily-pad, and stays: no gasping for air like a fish out of water, but he—or she—seems quite content looking upward at the sky. Ralph waits and watches and after a few minutes the tadpole squirms a bit and turns to face the other way, and one large eye looks back at Ralph like his puppy lying on the kitchen floor, head resting sideways on a paw as she looks upward to see if there's any food in the offing. Or perhaps the tadpole's looking at that blue sky, so different from the murky underwater view he's used to—this other world, so light and airy, around him.

Soon the tadpole shifts again, slips off the lily-pad, and is gone.

What I Wanted to Tell You

Yesterday, walking on the high banks of the Sucker River, I saw a deer far below me with three fawns, standing on a midriver sandbar. As I watched them, one of the fawns began to gambol and splash. Later I found the tiniest of toads, barely half an inch long. He had six pin-head spots on his back, rust-red like the pine needles he was sitting on. When I stood back up, a raven flew right overhead, circled around me several times, looking me over quite carefully. The bird was so close I could hear the sound of his wings through the air. The air was filled with late-summer light. *All is well,* the raven said, *the world is fine.*

Home Is Where the Art Is

Evening—the air is still, and the only sound I hear is the river far below me trickling over logs and sand. A half moon, behind a scrim of clouds, brightens in the southern sky. I sit beside a short, stout white pine, watching the river, and now I see a dark shape swimming against the current—beneath the water it seems as large as a dog—swimming with steady, sure strokes. . . .

Earlier this summer, wading in the river, I saw beneath a lip of bank, covered by undergrowth hanging down across it, an opening, round and dark, large enough for the dark shape I now see swimming upriver. "Bank beavers," the naturalist at Pictured Rocks called them, since instead of a lodge they live beneath the sandy banks, burrowing back from the river. I've seen the evidence: escape holes in the ground (sometimes ten or twenty feet away from the water), chewed-off stumps by the river's edge, brush piled against the bank (a food supply for the coming winter), and where I've broken a path along the bank, trees felled a day or two later to block the way. (These beaver trails are fine if you're a foot high—otherwise there's a lot of brush to get through.)

In the middle of a balsam thicket I stumbled one day upon a stump gnawed into the shape of a beaver. It's unmistakable: the squat form, hunched over, with forepaws held close to the chest, thick haunches for dragging logs or swimming upriver. This gnawed stump faces a huge white pine some thirty feet off—a self-portrait, perhaps, of the beaver I see this evening swimming in the river.

High in the southern sky a half moon breaks through the clouds. And the whippoorwills, one by one, begin to call into the night.

On the Last Day of Summer

On the last day of summer a raven did a barrel-roll in front of me. There I was in my canoe, paddling along—calm water in the cove, the September air still warm—when I heard croaking behind me, more drawn-out and extended than the usual guttural squawk that ravens speak with. Wondering what all the commotion was about, I looked up and saw a raven flying right above my head. Seconds later (and no more than a dozen feet in front of me), he tucked his wings in and rolled upside down, hanging for a moment in the air. I saw his feet sticking upward. Then, just before he began to drop, he righted himself and flew on.

Last Bird of the Season

A few days after the equinox, Ralph's surprised to see a sandpiper still poking around the sandbar near Towes Creek, though all weekend long a cold wind blew from the northwest, kicking Lake Superior up and dropping the temperature thirty degrees. "You're looking all bulked up, little guy," Ralph says, paddling past. Moments later, the bird skitters by Ralph and flies southward across the lake (the last he sees this year).

Only in Retrospect

It's only in retrospect that you can say, "This was the last warm day of the year"—sometime in early October, before the storm clouds come sweeping in across Lake Superior and the temperature drops twenty degrees in an hour. But yesterday was one such day, a mild wind blowing from the south, a few leaves dropping from the multi-colored trees.

More than a hundred crows flocked along the shore of Sable Lake, jawing back and forth into the morning air; two kingfishers flew upward into a cedar as I put my canoe into the water; out on the ruffled lake I saw a quintet of loons—flying south already?—and as I rounded the point near Towes Creek a bald eagle flew off from a maple and headed down the lake. Though the crows were all about, they hardly seemed to notice: a few made cursory passes toward the eagle but almost, it seemed, pro forma, cawing in mild dismay—nothing, to be sure, like the way they mobbed an owl roosting outside my bedroom window one morning last winter.

In the afternoon I took my dog up to the Sucker River, and as we approached the high banks a single raven across the valley took off and circled overhead. By then the wind had died (only hours later it had shifted to the north and was building toward thirty knots), and we could hear the river gurgling like a broken faucet beneath us. Before us and around us and across the valley the trees stood motionless in their red and orange party clothes. Having worked all summer to store up food, and having been released till spring from the need to make a living, they were at last free to lose their green and stand for all to see in their true, most personal finery.

After another week or two and a few more north winds, the revelry would be over and they would strip down and go to bed naked, to sleep it off beneath the winter's snows.

Ralph Wakes One Morning

Ralph wakes one morning to the sound of Canada geese flying south. The window is open this misty September morning, a three inch gap beneath the shade, and in his green room at six a.m. the distant honking is unmistakable: a large flock, high in the sky, strung out in an uneven line heading southwest. Actually Ralph sees out of one eye the pillow and a bit of open window above the radiator. When Ralph sticks his foot out, the radiator is warm.

Soon Ralph has lifted his head from the pillow, he's gotten out of bed and gone to the back door to let the dog out. Ralph puts water on for coffee and goes to the front door to let the dog back in and get the paper. The enormous maple down the street is still mostly green but going yellow around the edges. The small maple in front of it is already entirely orange.

Dear Martha, Ralph writes, sitting at his desk later with the light from the rainy September day casting itself softly over the yellow pad, *It's getting to be fall here and the trees down the street are already turning, we had such a cold summer and now as much rain as you must be getting on the west coast. . . .*

Ralph remembers flying over the Sierras that April and seeing out the window of the jet the full moon shining down on the snow-covered mountains. When he got to the San Francisco airport she was waiting for him, blue eyes the color of chicory and a purple leotard under her white shirt. He thought about going out the door with her and making love right there in the camper in the airport parking lot, as they swayed together and he smelled through her blond hair frangipani.

It took over three hours to get to the low mountain by the Russian River—the old Ford would hardly go fifty—back to her small house in the redwoods, a large wine vat someone had covered with a Plexiglas dome. The full moon shone through the enormous trees. They left the car by the side of the dirt road, walking the last hundred yards through a dew-soaked meadow. The chill of the night air settled on them. Ralph had been traveling all day.

By evening it has stopped raining and Ralph hears a squeak or two beyond the open window by his desk. He has been writing all day, one thing or another, proposals, critiques, correspondence—but his letter remains unfinished. Ralph notices that the bird feeder is empty, since the sparrows and chickadees have been feeding all morning and afternoon. Even in the rain they show up to eat and gossip. But the cardinal only comes at dusk, often when the feeder is empty, and though Ralph now goes out to fill it, the cardinal's a cautious bird and flies off when Ralph opens the back door.

When Ralph gets back to his desk he sees the cardinal has returned to the feeder. She's sitting there eating, looking up as she chews her sunflower seeds to watch the door and Ralph's window. Ralph hears in the quiet September evening the distinct sound of the cardinal cracking sunflower seeds. Slowly the air darkens. Soon, Ralph is sure, the single cricket in the catalpa out back will start his end-of-summer song.

Crow Story

The trees along the shore by Second Point are filled with crows. They've landed, the whole flock, a couple of hundred at least in the willows that line the shore. Rarely quiet, they are particularly vociferous today, talking back and forth, often at times leaping into the air, switching trees, always talking. . . .

What could it be they're talking about? I wonder, resting my paddle across the gunwales of my canoe. And now I see them one by one leaving the trees and dropping to the water's edge, where they stand on the sand (never more than a dozen at any time), half in the water, talking back and forth the whole time, and splash themselves . . . like my father used to do, throwing water back over his shoulders and under his arms, so as not to shock his heart in the cold Atlantic swells. (After a few minutes these crows fly up and preen themselves in the trees, while others take their place along the shore.)

Old Possum

The only marsupial in North America. Five toes on each foot; inside toe on hind foot opposable (an aid in climbing) and without claw. . . . Among the most primitive of living mammals. . . . May live seven years or more.
—Mammals (Peterson Field Guides)

Here's how it happens. The night before the full moon (the air still mild in October), while Ralph is walking his dog and the moon's shadows play under the oaks, he sees up the block, beneath the sole streetlight, just as his dog comes alert, an animal about the size of a large cat, with a pointed nose—and then it's gone and Ralph's dog is whining and straining at the leash.

The next morning, from his canoe out on the water, Ralph sees a possum by the shore, standing on a rock, face pointed downward. As Ralph moves closer, he sees that the creature's head is nodding like an old man falling asleep in his chair. When his nostrils hit the water, small bubbles appear on the lake's surface and the possum jerks his head up. As Ralph moves even closer, the animal senses his presence and raises his head, and Ralph sees that he's blind, no eyes left in his sockets, and yet he seems to have a clear idea of just where Ralph is, and starts to back up, the prehensile thumbs on his rear feet gripping the slick rock, appearing to Ralph as worn and lumpy as his father's hands before he died.

Later that day, walking his dog, Ralph sees that the possum has lain down in the water and is curled up with his head on a small rock and the gentle waves lapping his fur. At first Ralph thinks he's dead, but once again the creature must sense Ralph's presence—or smells his dog—and slowly he gets to his feet and faces them. Ralph withdraws, keeping his dog close by him on the leash, and the possum lies back down. A late bloom of algae by the water's edge covers the lower half of the possum in a pale green.

That night the full moon spreads its quicksilver across the lake, and the air is still mild. The next day, when Ralph walks his dog, the wind is blowing out of the northwest and there's a chill in the air. When Ralph gets to the lake's edge, he sees the rocks are empty. In the night, Ralph imagines, beneath the soft canopy of the full moon, the possum rose like

Elijah and, crossing the light-filled lake, ascended heavenward . . . while the autumn moon, a perfect circle of white, moved through the cloudless sky.

THREE:
WHAT THE RAVEN SAID

Ralph among the Buffleheads

Ralph turns his canoe where the willow stands next to the cotton-wood (both trees now bare of leaves), and starts for home. The wind has died. He paddles by three ducks on a rock, eyes closed: two males and a female, the males just now darkening to adulthood—they barely stir as Ralph passes by. Their breasts are stuffed with down like the parkas of Arctic explorers.

On his left he passes the limestone bluffs: Virginia creeper and rock honeysuckle are naked stems along the rock face. Down below, the lake slaps at the nooks and crannies it has hollowed out of the rock over many years. Ralph sees to his right the nose and back of a muskrat float-ing at ease on the calm water—and then as the merest breeze ripples the lake, Ralph sees the low log-like shapes of half-a-dozen carp feeding on the last algae of the year.

As Ralph gets closer to home, a flock of buffleheads fly in, all white and black like the lights and shadows of the Arctic where they summer. Today these ducks have brought the winter south: across the lake Ralph sees a white approaching mist—snow in the afternoon. (Having the longest journey south, these buffleheads are usually the last birds flying through, before the lake empties out for the winter.)

The Hills of the National Zoo

—for Marie

Magnolias and mourning doves on my mother's last birthday: it's
warm enough for a trip to the zoo, she in her wheelchair and wool jack-
et though I'm sleeveless and sweating, pushing the wheelchair up and
down the hills of the National Zoo. "When was the last time," I ask,
"someone took you to the zoo on your birthday?"
We pass by pampas grass on the sidewalk to the Language Lab, where
orangutans, longhair 'wild men' of the jungle, manipulate symbols for
praise: good boy . . . good girl—and a banana.

In front of us one female, facing us, watches as a teenager (there's a
visiting class here today) empties her purse. "Look at her eyes," my
mother says, "so deep and dark you could get lost in there."

*   *   *

Shortly after my mother died, I had a dream about her. She appeared
younger, healthier, as I remembered her in New York in the days when
she still had dark hair mixed in with the gray. She was wearing a long
wine-red winter coat and we were standing in the vestibule of a theater
which had been converted for use as a convention center. She had just
come in off the street. She was here for a meeting of some sort, and I
felt uncertain, like I did when I visited her once at the food pantry where
she volunteered after retiring from thirty-some years as a nutritionist.
She was in a hurry, in my dream, for this was a meeting of those new to
Death, and she had much to learn. She told me she was well, but very
busy. "I wish I could talk longer," she said, as she turned to the window-
less door which led into a meeting room.

And as for me, I told her, I was happy just to see her feeling better.

I Bury My Mother's Ashes

A year before she died, my mother visited me in Grand Marais, and I brought her to the high banks of the Sucker River. It was late evening, and we walked the few dozen yards from where I parked the car to where I'm standing now, looking down at the river. We stood there as the air grew dark around us—and then looking upward we saw five sandhill cranes gliding low overhead, heading to their nests a half mile south of here, where the trees give way to the sandy Whitewash plains.

I bury my mother's ashes up along the Sucker, in the same spot as my old dog, beneath a stout white pine. This tree was stunted early in life, but has grown out over the years and is now like the large flowering top of an ancient tree that's somehow been buried up to its neck in the sand of the high banks, so that its feet would be by the water's edge and my mother's ashes in the shade of its branches, looking out over the small river valley below.

Normally, there are few birds this late in the year, though today the air is mild. I've seen solitary ravens, and occasionally there's a nuthatch hidden in the pine, or a pair of chickadees. This day is different, however. Just as I step out to the overlook, a large red-tail hawk flies out from the top of the tall white pine down in the valley. At the same time two ravens fly across the valley squawking.

And this is just the beginning. After I place a small piece of granite over the pine needles that cover my mother's ashes, I begin to notice the birds. First a flock of cedar waxwings, gregarious as is their nature, follow me along the trail, so close I hear the rustling of their wings.

A flicker comes and sits on a branch not ten feet from me and, looking right at me, speaks to me in birdsong. I see many birds today I've never seen before and can't identify—which is not all that unusual, to be sure, though my mother would probably have known them all. As I stand looking out over the valley, another hawk drops out of a spruce and flies over the river. Since this hawk is actually below me, I can clearly see his reddish tail feathers.

And now a flock of crows flies into the valley. To be more accurate, they come in stages: first the advance scouts, who call back to their mates and alight on trees upstream. Then the others follow in waves, a few, a dozen, two dozen and more, cawing back and forth, settling for a while in the high branches of the pine and spruce, then continuing slowly southward until I can no longer see them. For a while longer I stand there, listening to their cries.

Mosquito Bay

The wind, the horn, the gulls: another rainy day on the Point. It's autumn now as I write, yellow leaves slipping by the window, these days growing shorter.

*　　*　　*

Tonight the wind has stopped. Out here on Coast Guard point, a sandy spit of land sticking into the cold blue of Lake Superior—and creating a harbor of refuge midway between Marquette and the Soo (in the last century and a half, many ships have gone down along this windy coast, attempting to make Mosquito Bay in a storm)—out here nothing grows but Balm-of-Gilead, on this sandy soil, really no soil at all, just sand. The large trees rustle in the slightest breeze, and the wind seems never to stop, constant, blowing off the lake (or rarely from the south: always, in that case, it seems, heavy with moisture—when there's a warm wind blowing across the bay, you can smell the damp pine forests).

Usually the wind is constant . . . but not tonight. When I wake, abruptly, I hear the silence. I put on a heavy wool shirt and go out on the porch. The leaves are still. Hours ago the moon has set, and the stars are brilliant above the dark water. Now I can hear the surf—waves rolling in from the northwest to crash on the sandy beach of East Bay. I stand on the porch overlooking the water and watch the northern lights pulsate across the sky "like God's own orgasm."

*　　*　　*

If you head north from Chicago, Mosquito Bay is about as far as you can get without crossing Lake Superior. Only a couple of hundred people live there, year round. It's one of the few places left in the U.S. where you can still call someone using only the last three digits of her phone number.

Empty stretches of café-au-lait sand beach surround the protected harbor, gulls turning above the water, spots of white against the spruce-and-pine forests. If it were any warmer, any other climate or location, a beach this white and sweeping would be jammed with bodies, the bay ringed with houses instead of dark forests that have trouble remembering the sun. Both Marquette and the Soo are more than a hundred miles away.

Red pine forests, ghosts of sun-light on the dune grass, the cry of the seagulls like children at play. Bleached drift-logs lie on the beach, torn from Lonesome Point in a November gale. All last night there was lightning but no rain—this morning, fog: you couldn't even see across the bay. Every fifteen seconds the foghorn sounds, a low bass note that echoes off the escarpment back of town.

✻   ✻   ✻

It's getting to be winter. One morning the bay is freezing, ice floating near the shore, even the gulls are gone. Silence. (Only a couple of crows and some sparrows are left from all the birds singing in June: the geese, the chorus of mourning doves, the gulls, the woodcock at dawn.)

A Four-Minute Mile Straight Uphill

At the base of the white pine is a small hole. For several years my dog has had a fondness for the squirrel who lives there, tucked away among the roots of the huge tree, which is, I'd say, at least 120 feet tall, far larger than any other here by the river, or, for that matter, any within a mile or two of this spot. At times, lying back on the pine needles with my head on a root of a neighboring tree, I've dozed off in the afternoon sun, only to be awakened by my dog's barking, as loud as if she'd smelled bear or moose—but I see, on looking around, a small reddish squirrel chattering away part way up the trunk. I think the squirrel enjoys playing these games of hide-and-seek.

I figure it like this: if the tree is 120 feet tall, which is twenty times my height, and the squirrel is six inches tall, one twelfth my height, then it's as though I were a squirrel looking up at 12 X 120 feet, or 1440 feet of tree. Yet this squirrel can run up the tree in less than a minute flat, judging by the time it takes for him to go partway up the trunk and then turn around to scold my dog—which would be like me running a four-minute mile straight uphill.

When the winter winds blow, and the tree is creaking far overhead, the squirrel is warm and comfortable in the pine-needle earth (covered by a blanket of insulating snow), dreaming perhaps of summertime, and of running skyward with a barking dog below.

What the Raven Said

Once there were wolves in the forest—and then the white folks came and cut the great pine for their homes in the city, and a wolf or moose these days is a rare sight in the scrubby brush that covers the sand. Only blackened stumps remain of the huge trees, "lighter-wood" that'll burn and burn in your campfire. And the river itself, the white men changed its path with dynamite and steam. They swerved it to empty twenty miles west, into the bay where their mills and steamers waited for wood—and now spoonful by spoonful, sand from the Whitewash plains fills the white folks' harbor.

All Souls' Day, Lake Superior State Forest

Before the Sucker flattens out for its run to Lake Superior, it first must make the plunge down from the Whitewash plains. In so doing it cuts a wide swath through the hundred feet of sand the glaciers left behind, a valley half a mile across. The river flows north through marshy bottomland that lies beneath the high sandy banks, ever shifting its contours and channels. Then the river changes course north-westward toward Perry's Landing. But just before the river turns to follow the path of least resistance, it narrows down abruptly, running faster now, more steeply, and cuts a ravine between two steep banks of white pine.

Years before the first logger came, when the glaciers were still melting, the river was higher by far and cut a deep bowl as it changed direction, and the great bowl-shaped basin is filled with ferns and maples. Now, at the beginning of November, the maple leaves are down but the ferns, oddly, are still green: acres of green ferns beneath the leafless trees. The sky is blue, the temperature still above freezing . . . before winter comes steaming down from Manitoba.

In the middle of this great fern-filled bowl is a steep mound that was once perhaps an island in the middle of the swirling river, though now the river flows murmuring along one side only, far down a precipitous sandy bank on top of which I've been eating lunch, sitting on a moss-covered pine stump. It must have been early in the logging years this tree was cut, because all around stand pines that are at least a century old themselves. After eating my cheese sandwich, I stand amidst the stillness and ask, out loud, "Is this far enough away for you?" Here where the river narrows and changes course, cutting its way down toward Lake Superior.

An Inch of Snow

There's about an inch of snow on the ground, and as dusk falls the snow holds the last daylight, and offers it back to the sky.

Paddler's Technique

Apart from the risk of drowning, hypothermia can quickly cause death to capsized canoeists . . . whenever the water temperature added to the air temperature gives a number lower than one hundred.
          —Guide to Canoeing (Wenonah Canoe Co.)

Ralph knows it's getting time to quit when he returns home one morning and the tip of the third finger of his left hand (that is, the third finger of his wetsuit glove, which covers a polypropylene liner, which covers his warm flesh) is covered with ice. Perhaps he should have known when he set out, since the air, though calm, was well below freezing, and Ralph had to break a thin layer of ice close to the shore before paddling. The water seems viscous at this temperature, like vodka left in a freezer, hard to push about with a paddle, hard to move through in a boat. The few miles that normally take Ralph an hour today take him nearly two.

So Ralph knows for sure it's time to quit when he gets back home and finds the tip of his finger encased in ice. Apparently this is all that touches the water (as he was taught, so many summer ago, that his fingers should just "kiss the water"), and, like a candle hand-dipped in tallow, each time Ralph slips his paddle through the water and lifts it back into the freezing air, another thin layer on his finger turns to ice—so that Ralph's third finger of his black neoprene wetsuit glove has a hard clear teardrop-shaped fingertip . . . which now, in the warmth of Ralph's mudroom, is slowly melting.

Last Canoe of the Season

Last canoe of the season: the rocks along the shoreline are sheathed in ice, and the lake itself is freezing over. Already ice extends twenty feet out from the shoreline, so that my canoe must serve as an icebreaker as I paddle out to open water, my paddle breaking the ice with each stroke. It's four o'clock in the afternoon and the setting sun gives a mild glow to the top of the oaks at Second Point. But the air, though still, is cold, and my hands are growing numb as I turn for home.

Now I see a large bird flying toward me along the shoreline, flapping too slowly to be a seagull, too steadily to be a red-tail hawk. Fifty yards away he turns and I see the white head and tail of a bald eagle. He hovers for a brief moment before setting off across the lake.

In a small cove near the end of the limestone bluffs, two ducks remain, sitting alongside each other on rocks that protrude from the ice close to shore. Perhaps they are the same pair I watched last spring, preening themselves on a log for nearly half an hour, before the drake slipped into the water and began swimming in lazy circles. After a short time the hen followed him and swam toward him—their heads bobbing at each other in slow syncopation. When they came together, he mounted her, nipping at the back of her head, and then only the top of her head and her eyes, and the nostrils at the top of her beak, remained above the water. After a few moments, he slipped off and swam around her, preening once again.

These ducks sit next to each other in the gathering dusk, facing outward across the lake. They will leave when there is no more open water—perhaps tomorrow. But for now they sit in the rose-colored dusk, watching as evening descends through the luminous wintry air.

The Ice like Crickets Singing

Walking down the front steps with my dog, going for our evening walk, I hear above me the sound of wings, and the clicking sounds that crows use with each other when they think that no one's listening. Looking up, I see two large black birds, one right above the other, wings flapping in unison, turning clockwise in a wide circle no more than forty feet above me. As I stand watching, they gain altitude, at times seeming to touch each other.

Then I see another pair of birds off to one side, who are doing the same strange dance. I stand looking upward, my dog whining at my feet. Slowly the birds climb, flapping steadily.

When the birds are several hundred feet in the air, and my neck is starting to ache from craning backward for so long, suddenly one breaks off from the others, and they begin to chase each other in a switch-and-run game of tag that I can't begin to follow—dark birds against a background of solid gray clouds. I hear them calling back and forth to each other. For a long while I stand there watching them against the clouds, and then they fly off southward until I can no longer make them out, though for a while longer I hear their calls.

All night long, ice is forming near the shore. A calm night, I can hear the ice scraping against itself, against the rocks—a sound like crickets on a summer night. These small noises fill the stillness of the night, as quiet as the raccoon climbing up over my balcony railing to eat the sunflower seeds I've left for her, fatter now than when I first saw her in the springtime. She's getting ready for winter's bloom of ice—which I can hear now, clearly, like crickets singing on the lake.

Now the Lake Is Empty

Now the lake is empty. The last ducks have left. Skinning the water's surface, so clear you can see the sandy lake bottom beneath it, is a thin green layer of ice. In this looking-glass you can see reflected the puffy white clouds motionless in the blue sky, like the depths of a lake you've never seen before. Here, at last, is a world you can learn to call your own.

About the Author

Robert Alexander grew up in Massachusetts. He attended the University of Wisconsin, and for several years taught in the Madison public schools. After receiving his Ph.D. in English from the University of Wisconsin at Milwaukee, he worked for many years as a freelance editor. He has previously published a book of poetry, *White Pine Sucker River: Poems 1970-1990* (New Rivers Press, 1993), and a book of creative non-fiction, *Five Forks: Waterloo of the Confederacy* (Michigan State University Press, 2003). From 1995 until 2001, he was a consulting editor at New Rivers Press, where he also served for two years as Creative Director. He is currently a contributing editor at White Pine Press, where he edits the Marie Alexander Poetry Series. He divides his time between southern Wisconsin and the Upper Peninsula of Michigan.

Author photo: David Tenenbaum